Mount Rushmore

by R.J. Bailey

National Park Service
U.S. Department of the Interior

Mount Rushmore National Memorial

Bullfrog Books

Ideas for Parents and Teachers

Bullfrog Books let children practice reading informational text at the earliest reading levels. Repetition, familiar words, and photo labels support early readers.

Before Reading

- Discuss the cover photo. What does it tell them?
- Look at the picture glossary together. Read and discuss the words.

Read the Book

- "Walk" through the book and look at the photos. Let the child ask questions. Point out the photo labels.
- Read the book to the child, or have him or her read independently.

After Reading

- Prompt the child to think more. Ask: Have you ever been to Mount Rushmore? Do you know whose faces are in the monument? What did they do?

Bullfrog Books are published by Jump!
5357 Penn Avenue South
Minneapolis, MN 55419
www.jumplibrary.com

Library of Congress Cataloging-in-Publication Data

Names: Bailey, R. J., author.
Title: Mount Rushmore / by R.J. Bailey.
Description: Minneapolis, Minnesota: Jump!, Inc., [2016] | Series: Hello, America! | Includes index.
Audience: Grades K-3.
Identifiers: LCCN 2016010029 (print)
LCCN 2016010398 (ebook)
ISBN 9781620313503 (hard cover: alk. paper)
ISBN 9781624963971 (e-book)
Subjects: LCSH: Mount Rushmore National Memorial (S.D.)—Juvenile literature.
Classification: LCC F657.R8 B35 2016 (print)
LCC F657.R8 (ebook) | DDC 978.3/93—dc23
LC record available at http://lccn.loc.gov/2016010029

Editor: Kirsten Chang
Series Designer: Ellen Huber
Book Designer: Molly Ballanger
Photo Researcher: Kirsten Chang

Photo Credits: All photos by Shutterstock except: Alamy, 20–21; AP Images, 16; arinahabich/123RF.com, 5; Corbis 14 (inset), 14–15; Getty Images, 10–11; Superstock, 18–19; Thinkstock, 6tl, 6tr, 13, 23br.

Printed in the United States of America at Corporate Graphics in North Mankato, Minnesota.

Table of Contents

Mountain Faces

We are at Mount Rushmore.
It is in South Dakota.

Look up. What do you see?
Faces. Wow!

Who are they?
U.S. presidents.

The mountain
is a monument.

It helps us
remember four
great men.

Almost 400 people worked on it.

When did they start?

In 1927.

They blasted away rock.
Boom!

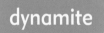

dynamite

How?

They used dynamite.

They used tools
to make the faces.

When was it done?

In 1941.

Today, rangers take care of it.

They climb high.

They fill gaps in the rock.

Jo is a ranger. She greets us.

Hi, Jo!

We walk by
a lot of flags.

There is one
for each state.

Let's take a picture!

We had fun at
Mount Rushmore.

21

Presidents of Mount Rushmore

Thomas Jefferson was president from 1801 to 1809. He wrote the Declaration of Independence, which said America was free from England.

Theodore Roosevelt was president from 1901 to 1909. He protected land all over the country to become national parks.

George Washington was president from 1789 to 1797. He was the country's first president.

Abraham Lincoln was president from 1861 to 1865. He signed the Emancipation Proclamation, freeing slaves in the United States.

Picture Glossary

dynamite
A powerful explosive used in blasting and mining.

presidents
The people who serve in the highest office in the United States.

monument
Something built to remember a person or event.

South Dakota
A state in the north-central United States.

Index

To Learn More

Learning more is as easy as 1, 2, 3.

1) Go to www.factsurfer.com

2) Enter "MountRushmore" into the search box.

3) Click the "Surf" button to see a list of websites.

With factsurfer.com, finding more information is just a click away.